# Let's Learn FRENCH Coloring Book

### Anne-Françoise Hazzan

**PASSPORT BOOKS**

*NTC/Contemporary Publishing Group*

**Library of Congress Cataloging-in-Publication Data**
is available from the United States Library of Congress.

Published by Passport Books,
a division of NTC/Contemporary Publishing Group, Inc.,
4255 West Touhy Avenue,
Lincolnwood (Chicago), Illinois 60712-1975 U.S.A.
© 1986 by NTC/Contemporary Publishing Group, Inc.
International Standard Book Number: 0-8442-1389-6

0 1 2 3 4 5 6 7 8 9 ML 19 18 17 16 15 14 13 12

# l'alphabet

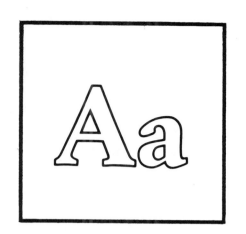

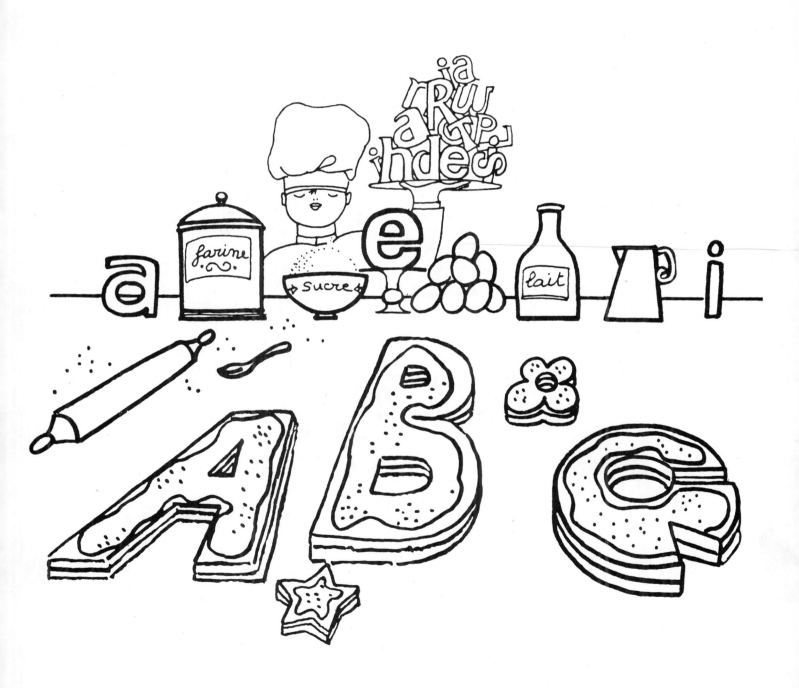

# A a

## *les animaux*

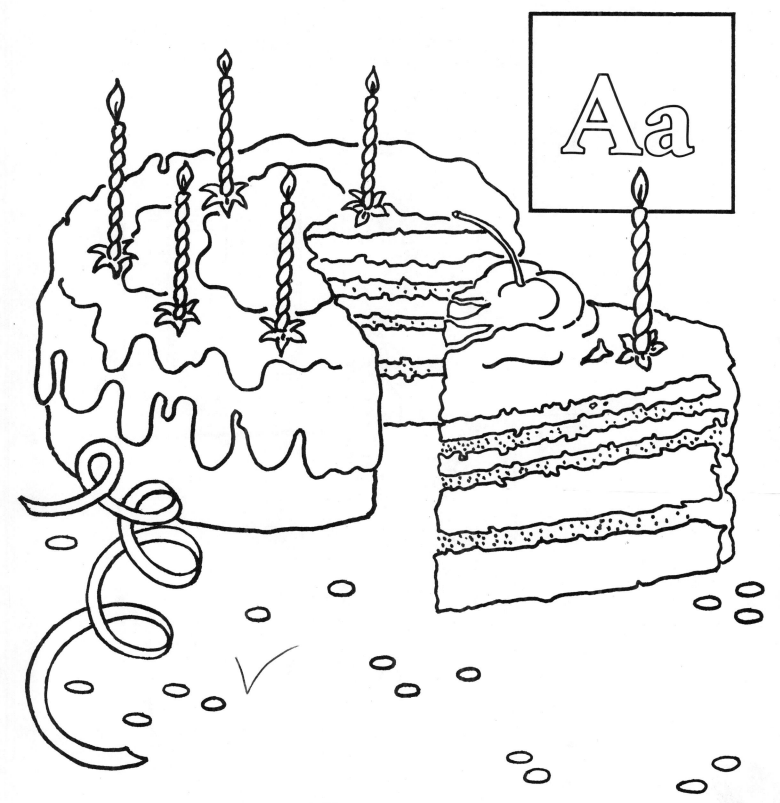

A a

l'anniversaire

# Aa

## l'automne

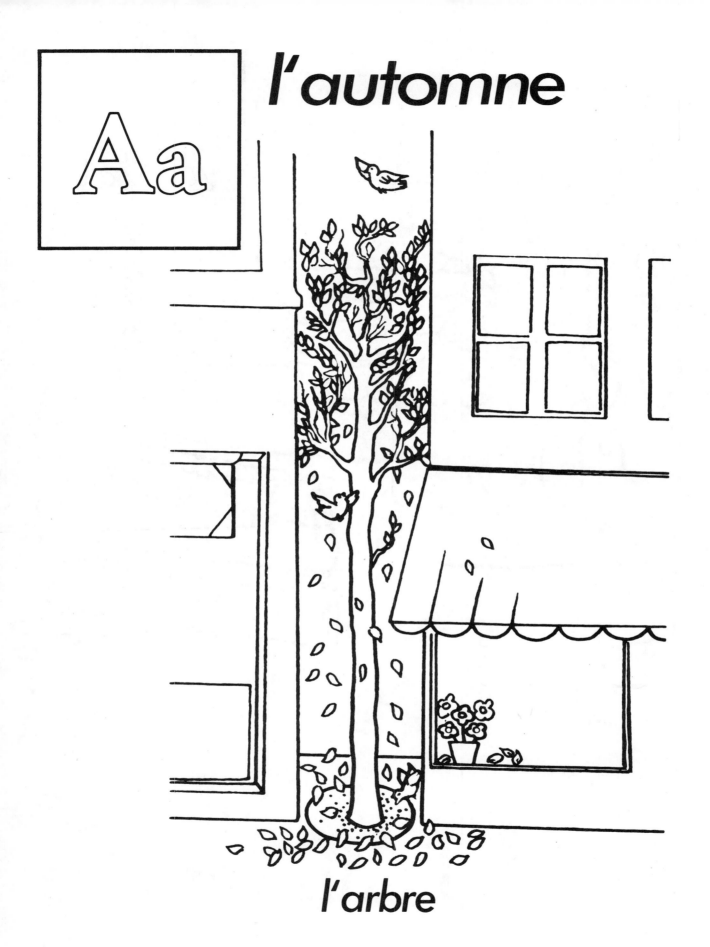

l'arbre

*le bateau*

**Bb**

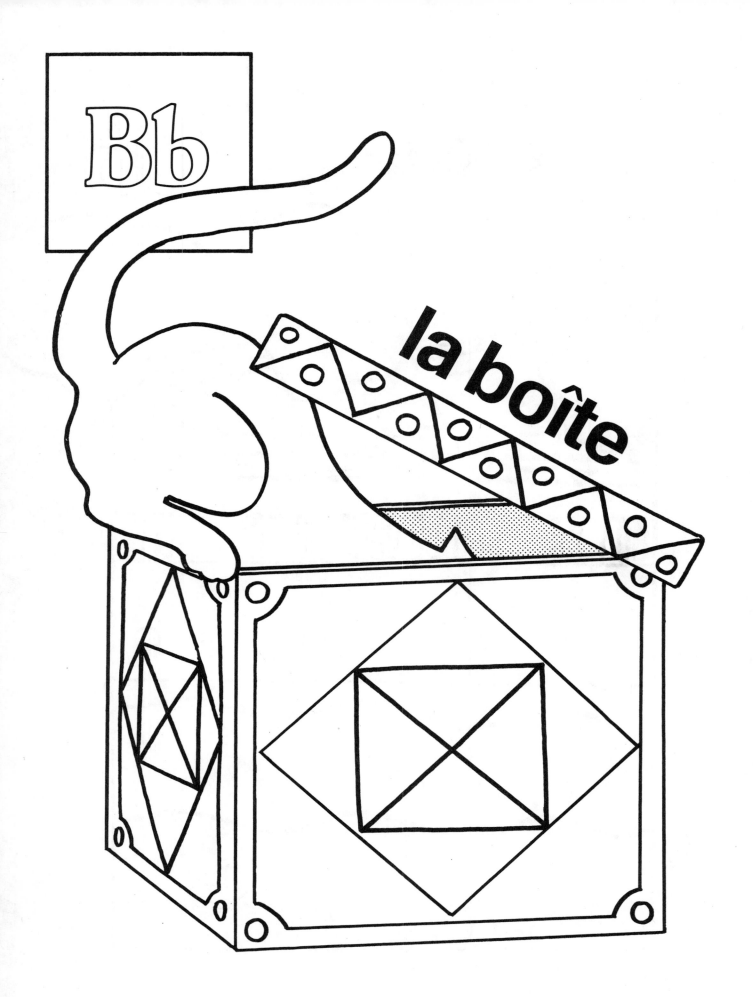

**Bb**

la boîte

# le bonbon

**Cc**

le cadeau

le chat

C c

la souris

**Cc**

le chien

le coq

**D d**

*le dragon*

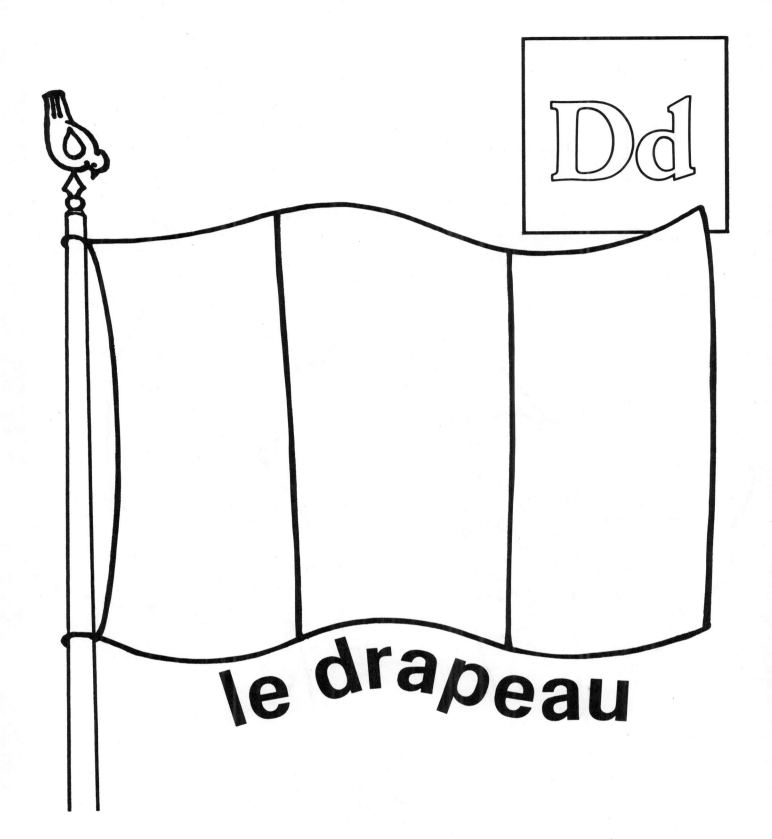

**le drapeau**

D d

**E e**

*l'éléphant*

# l'été

Ee

# Ff

**la fleur**

# la France

## Ff

*les fruits*

# Hh

l'heure

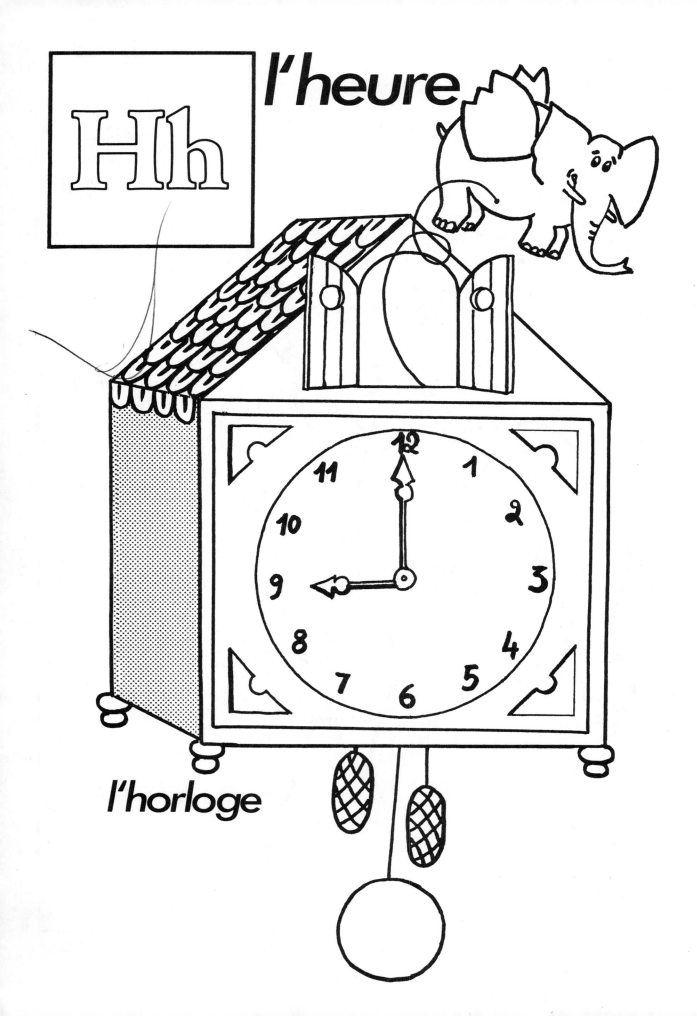

l'horloge

l'hiver

Hh

**l'île**

# l'immeuble

**I i**

# J j

## le jardin

la carotte

la tomate

**les jouets**

# Kk

le kangourou

# le kilo

**Kk**

le poisson

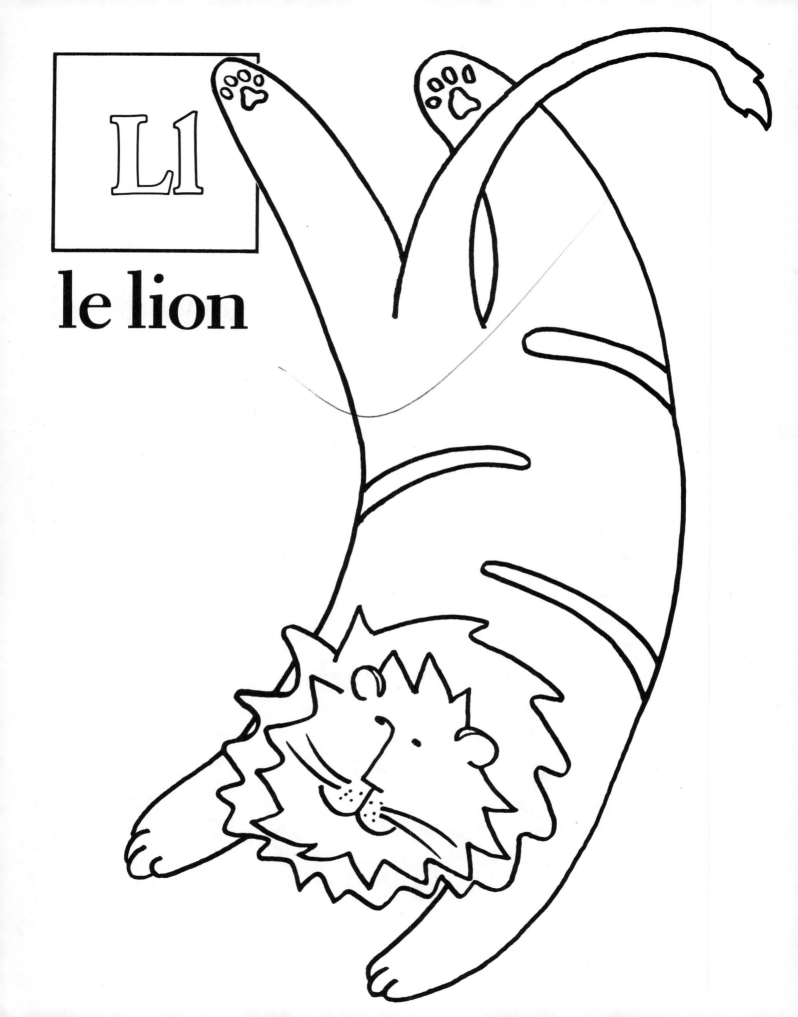

L1

le lion

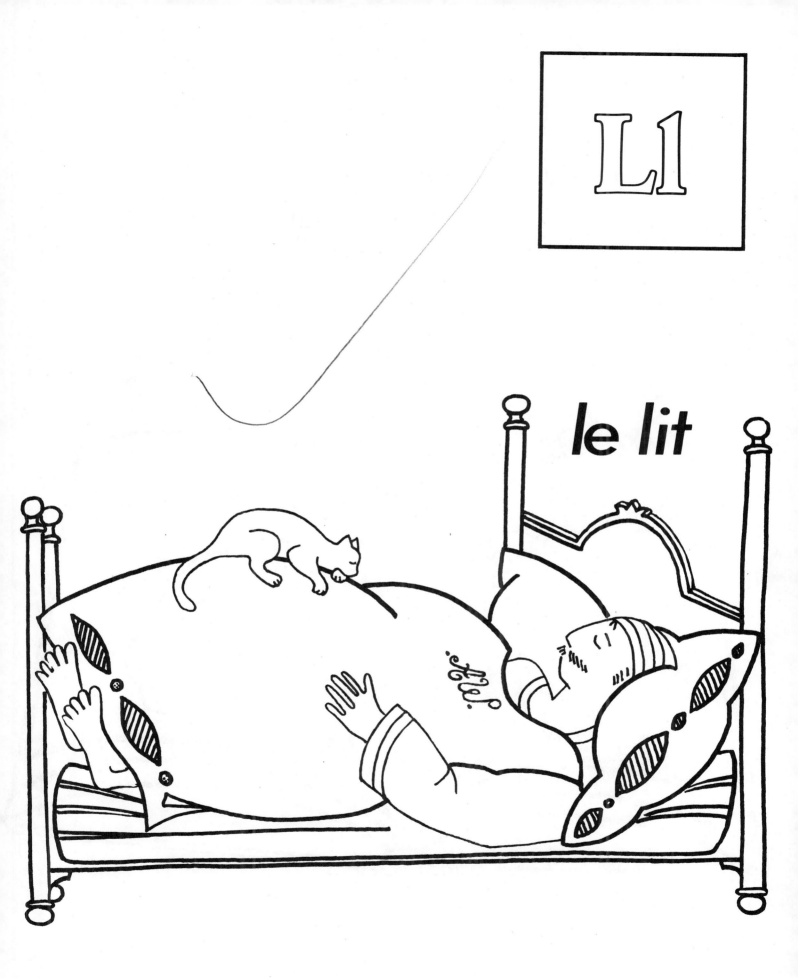

L1

le lit

# le livre

**M m**

*la maison*

**Mm**

la mère

*la neige*

# les nombres

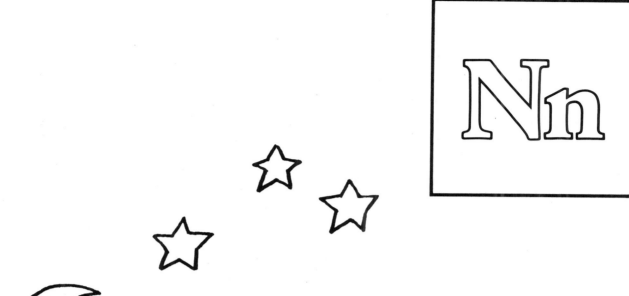

# Nn

*la nuit*

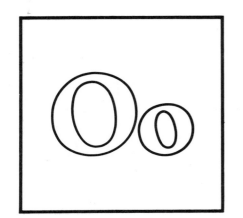

*l'oiseau*

# l'opéra

**Oo**

*la ballerine*

**P p**

le papillon

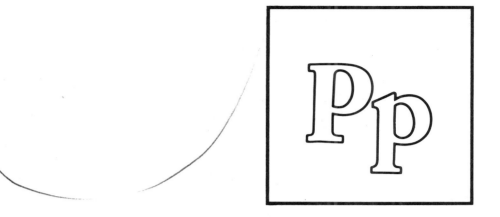

**Paris**

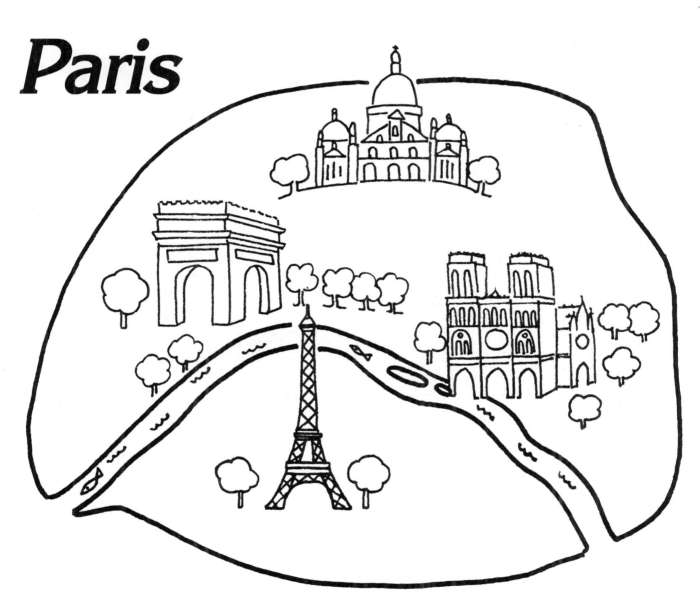

P p

le père

le bébé

# le printemps

P p

# Qq

## le Québec

JE ME SOUVIENS

Rr

le repas

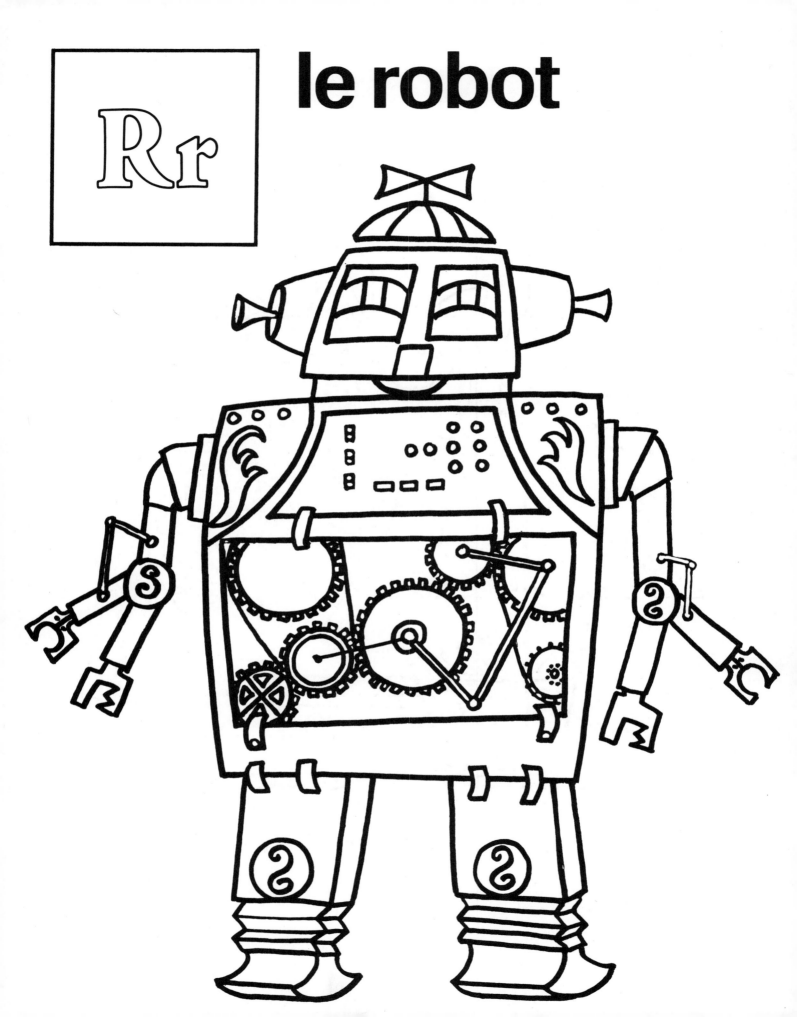

# le robot

le roi

**Rr**

la reine

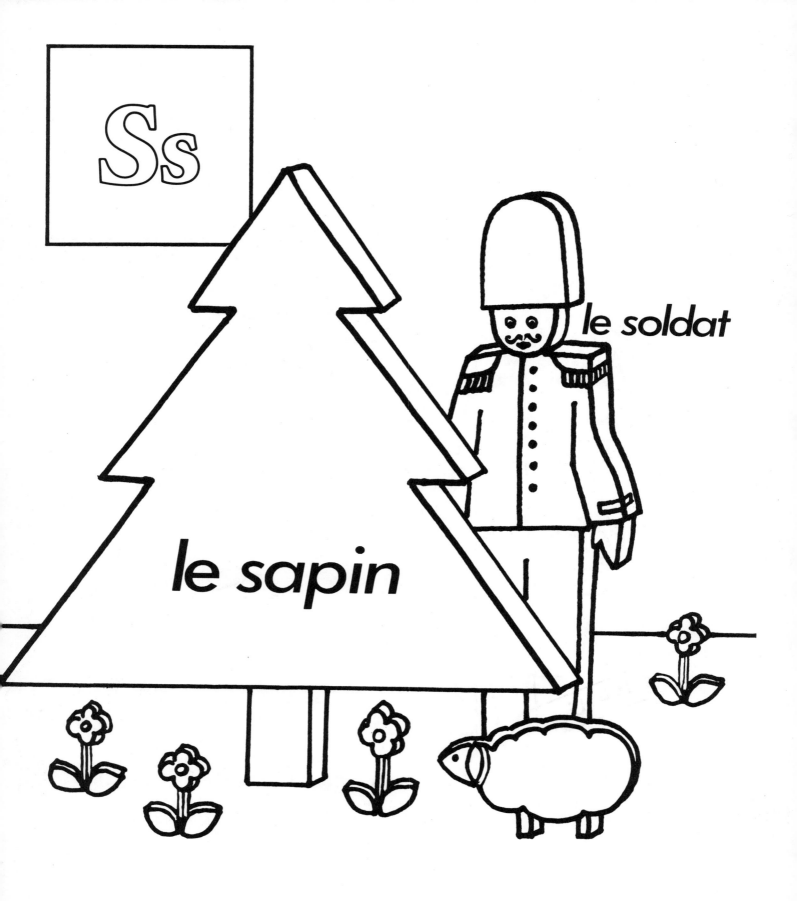

**S s**

**le soldat**

**le sapin**

# la semaine

# Ss

## la sirène

Ss

le soleil

la lune

Tt

tarte
aux fruits

la tarte

*la terre*

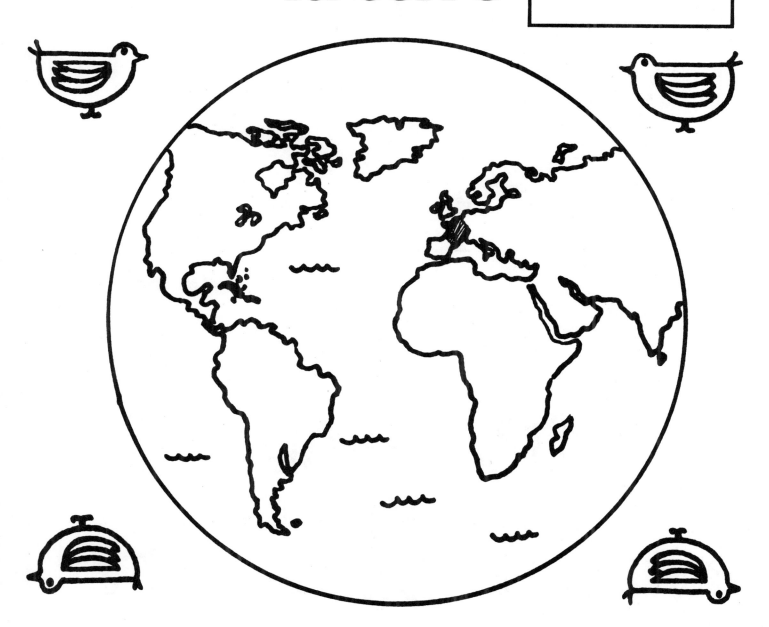

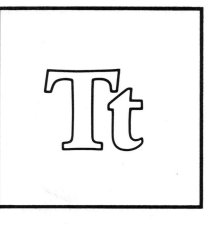

# Tt

le trésor

# les uniformes

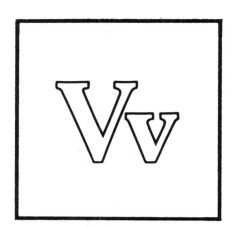

## les vêtements

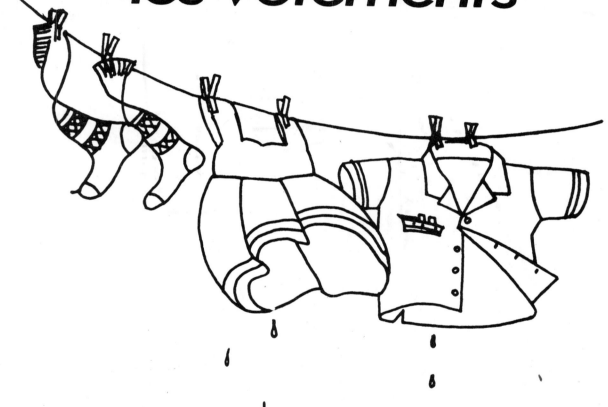

# la voiture

**W w**

*le wagon*

le wagon

le xylophone

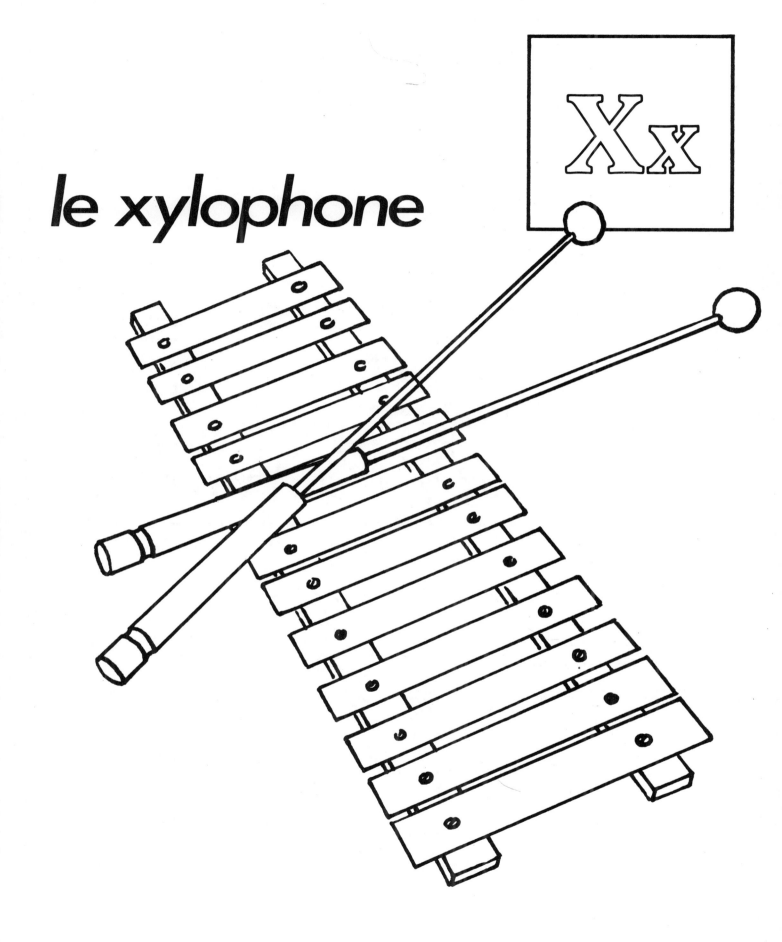

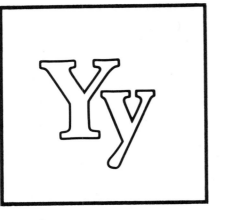

# le yogourt

# le zèbre

**Zz**

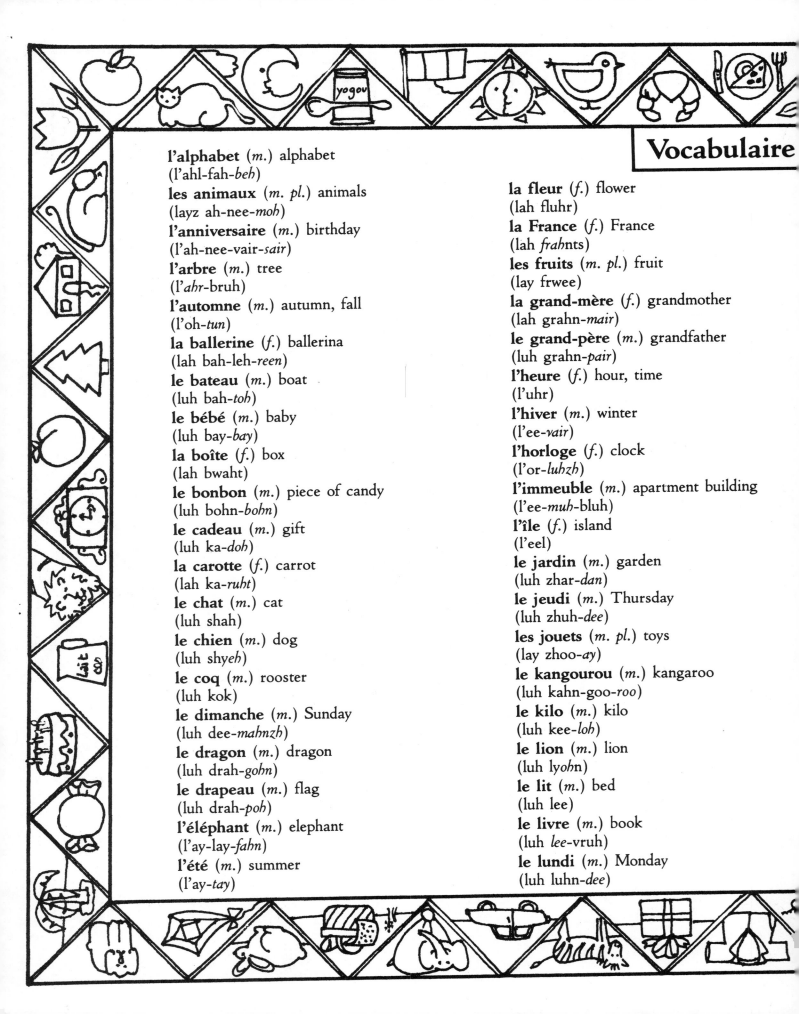

# Vocabulaire

**l'alphabet** (*m.*) alphabet
(l'ahl-fah-*beh*)

**les animaux** (*m. pl.*) animals
(layz ah-nee-*moh*)

**l'anniversaire** (*m.*) birthday
(l'ah-nee-vair-*sair*)

**l'arbre** (*m.*) tree
(l'*ahr*-bruh)

**l'automne** (*m.*) autumn, fall
(l'oh-*tun*)

**la ballerine** (*f.*) ballerina
(lah bah-leh-*reen*)

**le bateau** (*m.*) boat
(luh bah-*toh*)

**le bébé** (*m.*) baby
(luh bay-*bay*)

**la boîte** (*f.*) box
(lah bwaht)

**le bonbon** (*m.*) piece of candy
(luh bohn-*bohn*)

**le cadeau** (*m.*) gift
(luh ka-*doh*)

**la carotte** (*f.*) carrot
(lah ka-*ruht*)

**le chat** (*m.*) cat
(luh shah)

**le chien** (*m.*) dog
(luh shy*eh*)

**le coq** (*m.*) rooster
(luh kok)

**le dimanche** (*m.*) Sunday
(luh dee-*mahnzh*)

**le dragon** (*m.*) dragon
(luh drah-*gohn*)

**le drapeau** (*m.*) flag
(luh drah-*poh*)

**l'éléphant** (*m.*) elephant
(l'ay-lay-*fahn*)

**l'été** (*m.*) summer
(l'ay-*tay*)

**la fleur** (*f.*) flower
(lah fluhr)

**la France** (*f.*) France
(lah *frah*nts)

**les fruits** (*m. pl.*) fruit
(lay frwee)

**la grand-mère** (*f.*) grandmother
(lah grahn-*mair*)

**le grand-père** (*m.*) grandfather
(luh grahn-*pair*)

**l'heure** (*f.*) hour, time
(l'uhr)

**l'hiver** (*m.*) winter
(l'ee-*vair*)

**l'horloge** (*f.*) clock
(l'or-*luhzh*)

**l'immeuble** (*m.*) apartment building
(l'ee-*muh*-bluh)

**l'île** (*f.*) island
(l'eel)

**le jardin** (*m.*) garden
(luh zhar-*dan*)

**le jeudi** (*m.*) Thursday
(luh zhuh-*dee*)

**les jouets** (*m. pl.*) toys
(lay zhoo-*ay*)

**le kangourou** (*m.*) kangaroo
(luh kahn-goo-*roo*)

**le kilo** (*m.*) kilo
(luh kee-*loh*)

**le lion** (*m.*) lion
(luh ly*ohn*)

**le lit** (*m.*) bed
(luh lee)

**le livre** (*m.*) book
(luh *lee*-vruh)

**le lundi** (*m.*) Monday
(luh luhn-*dee*)

# Vocabulary

**la lune** (*f.*) moon
(lah loon)

**la maison** (*f.*) house
(lah meh-*zohn*)

**le mardi** (*m.*) Tuesday
(luh mahr-*dee*)

**le mercredi** (*m.*) Wednesday
(luh mair-kruh-*dee*)

**la mère** (*f.*) mother
(lah mair)

**la neige** (*f.*) snow
(lah nezh)

**les nombres** (*m. pl.*) numbers
(lay *nohm*-bruh)

**la nuit** (*f.*) night
(lah nwee)

**l'oiseau** (*m.*) bird
(l'wa-*zoh*)

**l'opéra** (*m.*) opera house
(l'oh-pay-*rah*)

**le papillon** (*m.*) butterfly
(luh pah-pee-*yohn*)

**Paris** (*m.*) Paris
(pah-*ree*)

**le père** (*m.*) father
(luh pair)

**le poisson** (*m.*) fish
(luh pwah-*sohn*)

**le printemps** (*m.*) spring
(luh pran-*tohn*)

**le Québec** (*m.*) Quebec
(luh kay-*behk*)

**le repas** (*m.*) meal
(luh ruh-*pah*)

**le robot** (*m.*) robot
(luh roh-*boh*)

**la reine** (*f.*) queen
(lah rehn)

**le roi** (*m.*) king
(luh rwah)

**le samedi** (*m.*) Saturday
(luh sahm-*dee*)

**le sapin** (*m.*) Christmas tree
(luh sah-*pan*)

**la semaine** (*f.*) week
(lah suh-*mehn*)

**la sirène** (*f.*) mermaid
(lah see-*rehn*)

**le soldat** (*m.*) soldier
(luh sohl-*dah*)

**le soleil** (*m.*) sun
(luh soh-*lay*)

**la souris** (*f.*) mouse
(lah soo-*ree*)

**la tarte** (*f.*) tart; pie
(lah tahrt)

**la terre** (*f.*) earth
(lah tair)

**la tomate** (*f.*) tomato
(lah toh-*maht*)

**le trésor** (*m.*) treasure
(luh tray-*zohr*)

**les uniformes** (*f. pl.*) uniforms
(layz oo-nee-*fohrm*)

**le vendredi** (*m.*) Friday
(luh vohn-druh-*dee*)

**les vêtements** (*m. pl.*) clothing
(lay veht-*mohn*)

**la voiture** (*f.*) car
(lah vwah-*toor*)

**le wagon** (*m.*) railroad car
(luh va-*gohn*)

**le xylophone** (*m.*) xylophone
(luh zee-loh-*fuhn*)

**le yogourt** (*m.*) yoghurt
(luh yoh-*goor*)

**le zèbre** (*m.*) zebra
(luh *zeh*-bruh)

# How Much Have You Learned?

Try to remember the French word as you color each picture.